1

Our Daily Bread:
Scriptures and Reflections for Life

Written by
Richard Tew

Our Daily Bread: Scriptures and Reflections for Life

Written by Richard Tew

Cover and page art by Avery Chumley

Editing by Pastor Mark Fleming

Forward

In the rhythm of our busy lives, it can be easy to forget the simple truth that God's Word is meant to be lived, not just read. Our Daily Bread: Scriptures and Reflections for Life byRichard Tew, is an invitation to slow down, to draw near to God, and to rediscover the peace, strength, and hope that only His word can provide.
Each page in this collection pairs scripture with heartfelt reflection; a gentle reminder that faith is not confined to Sunday mornings, but is woven through every joy, sorrow,and challenge we face.

These meditations illuminate how God's promises speak into the realities of our daily walk: to love when it's hard, toforgive when it hurts, to trust when life feels uncertain, and to find gratitude even in seasons of waiting.

The passages gathered here timeless verses from across the Bible remind us that we are not alone on this journey. The same God who strengthened Joshua, comforted David and redeemed Paul, continues to sustain and guide us today.
Each reflection serves as a quiet conversation betweenthe Creator and His creation: a whisper of grace, a spark of conviction, a word of encouragement to carry throughthe day.

May these scriptures and thoughts awaken a deeper desire within you to walk with God daily, to see His hand in the ordinary and to live out your faith with renewed courage andcompassion. As you read, pause and listen. Let His Word speak to your heart. For it is in His Word that we find our purpose, our peace, and our daily bread.

Jonathan Sanford, Evangelist

This book is in honor of my family and their profound faith tradition they have shared with me since I was a child. It is also a tribute to Becca, without her, the idea for these scriptures and reflections would have never started some eight years ago. It's also a "thank you" to Matt, who was willing to take a chance on me and put faith back on the radio, giving a voice to this project for all to hear.

Luke 6:27
"But I say unto you which hear, love your enemies,
do good to them which hate you."

It's hard to love our enemies. Jesus, the creator and perfect or of our faith did just that. In this verse, Jesus tells usto love our enemies and to extend grace to those who hurtus. It reminds us as much as people's misdeeds can hurt us, our sin hurts the lord. God's love fills our hearts and helps us through his Holy Spirit. History is replete with examples of how God's abundant love and grace can change even the most hardened of hearts. The love and grace we show othersshould serve as a reminder of how much God love us.

2 Corinthians 9:8

"And God is able to make all grace abound toward you; that ye,
always having all sufficiency in all things,
may abound to every good work."

This verse reminds us as believers about the sufficiency of God, and his will for us as his children.

We might wantan expensive car when what we really need is reliable transportation to get us to and from work each day.

The second part of the passage describes a promise betweenGod and his children that he can and will bless them beyond their understanding if they are both faithful to him, and honor him in their daily lives.

Isaiah 43:25

"I, even I, am he that blotteth out thy transgressions for mine own sake, and will not remember thy sins."

We all sin and transgress against God. He reminded the Jewish people only he could forgive them of their unrighteousness, and he promised them forgiveness when they returned to him.

In the book of Matthew, there are parallels to the same promise Jesus would later make to his early followers. It reminded members of the early church (and to us) that despite our faults and imperfections, through repentance, a sincere believer can find true forgiveness and peace once again.

John 16:33

"These things I have spoken unto you, that in me ye might have peace. In the world ye shall have tribulation: but be of good cheer; I have overcome the world."

In this verse, Jesus tells us it is our faith in him and his atoning sacrifice which gives us a sense of peace and assurance in life.

Jesus also reminds us he has overcome the temptations of the world; something we could never do on our own. In this scripture, Jesus is reminding us of the challenges and temptations we are sure to face as believers.

His resurrection shows us we can have hope through our faith in him and his finished work on the cross.

Isaiah 41:10

"Fear thou not; for I am with thee: be not dismayed; for I am thy God: I will strengthen thee; yea, I will help thee; yea, I will uphold thee with the right hand of my righteousness."

When uncertainty comes, fear can become more and more a part of our lives. If left unchecked, it can feel as if it is paralyzing us. Job loss, heartache over relationships, sickness, financial problems and the like can lead us to fear and dismay. God offers help, and promises us he will uphold us in his "righteous right hand;" a symbol of strength in times past. He reminds us he is always nearby, and through our faith in him will never leave or forsake us.

Philippians 4:6-7

"Be careful for nothing; but in everything by prayer and supplication with thanksgiving let your requests be made known unto God. And the peace of God, which passeth all understanding, shall keep your hearts and minds through Christ Jesus."

Life's challenges can—and often times do—make us anxious.

In this scripture, Paul exhorts believers to pray and petition God not just for an outcome which benefits us, but an one which glorifies our heavenly father.

The second part of the verse assures the believer this peace which "passeth all understanding" will guard both our hearts and minds in Jesus Christ.

Psalms 34:6-8

"This poor man cried, and the Lord heard him, and saved him out of all his troubles. The angel of the Lord encampeth round about them that fear him, and delivereth them. O taste and see that the Lord is good: blessed is the man that trusteth in him."

This scripture encapsulates the love of God to the faithful.

When the poor man in this story called out to God, he heard him. The verse goes on to show how God sends angels to those who fear him in order to deliver them from their troubles. We are reminded that the Lord is good, and we as believers can find safety when we abide in Him each and every day.

Romans 8:28

"And we know that all things work together for good to them that love God, to them who are the called according to his purpose."

This verse is specific to those who love God, and highlights his role in helping his children throughout their lives. It emphasizes the father's desire to unite with believers through their faith in order to live a life of righteousness. It offers hope to believers and reminds us that despite our failings, whatever we endeavor to do can be used to glorify God.

Joshua 1:9

"Have not I commanded thee? Be strong and of a good courage; be not afraid, neither be thou dismayed: for the Lord thy God is with thee whithersoever thou goest."

In this scripture, Joshua was being tested by God.

In some ways, it was a test of his faith, a faith he would need in order to lead God's people to the promised land. Joshua faced many unknowns as he guided the Israelites to Canaan. Still, his faith led him onward. God speaks to us in the same way he spoke to Joshua so many years ago. He reminds the believer to not be frightened or dismayed, but to cling to the Lord throughout life's trials and tribulations.

Galatians 5:6

"For in Jesus Christ neither circumcision availeth anything, nor uncircumcision; but faith which worketh by love."

This passage confirms it's not tradition or works of the law that sanctifies us. Rather, a believer in Jesus is one who has placed their faith in the Lord and his death upon the cross.

We should always labor to follow his examples highlighted through his teachings. Chiefly of among them is love for God and also for others. It's a believer's faith which serves as an attachment to Christ, one that prompts them to follow and be obedient to him.

True faith engenders and motivates us to seek the will of God. Embracing the love and grace of Jesus, the perfect or of our faith, helps us find the peace and happiness we continually search for in this life.

Isaiah 40:31

"But they that wait upon the Lord shall renew their strength; they shall mount up with wings as eagles; they shall run, and not be weary; and they shall walk, and not faint."

Hope. It's something we depend on to get through the toughest days and nights.

The author of Isaiah tells us we can lean on the Lord our God for our struggles, and as a resource for our strength. This scripture describes the faithful in metaphorical terms like eagles renewing their strength by placing their hope in God.

This verse reminds us of the strength and hope we can find for our daily struggles through our faith in God and his everlasting love for us.

2 Peter 1:5-7

"And beside this, giving all diligence, add to your faith virtue; and to virtue knowledge; And to knowledge temperance; and to temperance patience; and to patience godliness; And to godliness brotherly kindness; and to brotherly kindness charity."

In this passage, the author is describing the building blocks of the Christian faith: goodness, knowledge, self-control, perseverance, godliness, affection and love. Each attribute is used to build upon the next. There is a clear line connecting these aspects of the Christian faith. God wants each believer to "make every effort" to develop their faith in order to be exemplars of Christ to those around us in our lives.

Matthew 5:14-16

"Ye are the light of the world. A city that is set on a hill cannot be hid. Neither do men light a candle, and put it under a bushel, but on a candlestick; and it giveth light unto all that are in the house. Let your light so shine before men, that they may see your good works, and glorify your Father which is in heaven."

In this scripture, Jesus is telling his followers they are the light of the world. He reminds them they were indwelled with the Holy Spirit, and should bear light and produce fruit for the kingdom of heaven. We are reminded our example is always on display, not just in church or around our friends but in public for all to see.

2 Timothy 1:7

"For God hath not given us the spirit of fear; but of power, and of love, and of a sound mind."

In this scripture, the Apostle Paul tells Timothy, a student of Paul, to teach these important aspects of faith to the fledgling church he was shepherding. God does not give us a spirit of fear. Said another way, the father empowers us to overcome, to push on, to get up when we fall. He does this through his Holy Spirit. A gift all believers is given when they trust in the finished work of Jesus on the cross. The responsibility of each believer is to learn to use this internal strength with love and self-control.

Psalms 37:4

"Delight thyself also in the Lord: and he shall give thee the desires of thine heart."

In this scripture, King David, the author of the book of Psalms, is exhorting the reader to ingratiate themselves with God's love and purpose, not in earthly treasures. Chasing money and other temporary desires of the flesh doesn't bring lasting happiness or contentment. It only succeeds in engendering an insatiable quest for more and more, leaving the believer to follow an endless cycle of self-gratification while never finding the true peace in life only God can give.

The "desires of the heart" mentioned at the end of the verse refer to God granting us our desires only when they align with his will and purpose for us.

Matthew 11:28-30

"Come unto me, all ye that labor and are heavy laden, and I will give
you rest. Take my yoke upon you, and learn of me; for I am meek
and lowly in heart: and ye shall find rest unto your souls.
For my yoke is easy, and my burden is light."

This passage teaches us as believers we can find refuge in Jesus. Our weakness becomes our strength through Christ's sacrifice. He tells us his yoke, which is our decision to believe in and follow him, is light, not heavy. Jesus reminds us of his gentleness and purity of heart.

These characteristics are what we as his followers are to strive to emulate each day. We can take hope in the fact Jesus comforts our fears, and helps us overcome our challenges and burdens as he labors with us every step of the way.

Mark 11:24

"Therefore I say unto you, what things so ever ye desire, when ye pray, believe that ye receive them, and ye shall have them."

This passage shows Jesus emphasizing faith through the medium of prayer.

Many people read this verse and think Jesus will give them whatever they want as long as they pray for it. This passage implies Jesus is talking about using prayer for things which help us in our spiritual life not just our material needs and wants. He is trying to teach his followers about the faith aspect of prayer. The trust faith requires, the manifestation of our deep belief in God and his ability to help us not just in times of need but at whatever stage in life our prayerful requests might find us.

Hebrews 11:1

"Now faith is the substance of things hoped for, the evidence of things not seen."

This passage of scripture addresses the essence of what it means to be a Christian: one's personal faith. In this context, faith is not just a simple belief in what we want to be true. Rather, it's a confidence binding all aspects of life to the believer. It's an immeasurable trust in God to direct our path towards living out a life of service to him. As one commenter put it: "Faith proves to the mind, the reality of things that cannot be seen by the bodily eye." It's this deep, intrinsic faith which leads the Christian onward despite doubts and fears, to an ever-increasing sense of unity with God through his son Jesus Christ.

Luke 6:38

"Give, and it shall be given unto you; good measure, pressed down, and shaken together, and running over, shall men give into your bosom. For with the same measure that ye measure with it shall be measured to you again."

In this scripture, Jesus is telling his disciples about God's grace and the blessings afforded to each believer. He's also telling his flock in order to receive, they would first give. They are to show the generosity they have received from God, which he first gave them. Applying this scripture to us, Jesus isn't telling us to give arbitrarily just so we can receive material blessings. He tells us to give in order to help others and to bring glory to the Father for all he has given to us.

Proverbs 3:25-26

"Be not afraid of sudden fear, neither of the desolation of the wicked, when it cometh. For the Lord shall be thy confidence, ands hall keep thy foot from being taken."

How many times have we found ourselves facing something we never expected? It's impossible to prepare for life's unknowns, but we can have hope knowing whatever may come our way. Our Lord the rock of our faith is with us.

The unbeliever has no such hope. They are easily tossed to and fro by the tumultuous winds of change. The faithful have an anchor. Jesus has endured more than we can imagine and rose victorious on the other side. He offers us his hand to guide us through any challenge we may face, and offers us hope through our faith in him and his purpose for us.

Galatians 5:1

"Stand fast therefore in the liberty wherewith Christ hath made us free, and be not entangled again with the yoke of bondage."

This passage finds the Apostle Paul teaching the new Christians of his day about being freed from a life full of rituals and ceremonies under the old law. "Slavery" as Paul put it, was the indebtedness these new believers found themselves under the Mosaic law with its onerous requirements. Paul's message and its application for us is the same. Our hope galvanized and strengthened by our faith in Jesus' atoning sacrifice for our sins is an all-encompassing sacrifice which grants us the freedom the old law could never give.

1 John 4:16-17

"And we have known and believed the love that God hath to us. God is love; and he that dwelleth in love dwelleth in God, and God in him. Herein is our love made perfect, that we may have boldness in the day of judgment: because as he is, so are we in this world."

This scripture emphasizes love, and how the creator and his creation are to be connected through it. Elsewhere in scripture, Jesus says the "greatest commandment" is to love your neighbor as yourself. Its clear love is to be at the center of a believer's life and evidenced in all they do. It's through this prism of love we are to live our lives and be united with God through Jesus Christ.

Philippians 2:1-4

"If there be therefore any consolation in Christ,
if any comfort of love, if any fellowship of the Spirit, if any bowels
and mercies, Fulfil ye my joy,
that ye be likeminded, having the same love, being of one accord, of
one mind. Let nothing be done through strife or vainglory; but in
lowliness of mind let each esteem other better
than themselves. Look not every man on his own things, but every
man also on the things of others."

In this scripture, the Apostle Paul is telling believers in Phillipi they should emulate Christ's life through love; living through the Holy Spirit and considering others over themselves. We would do well to apply this scripture to our own lives by living a life of love and selflessness to the honor and glory of our Lord Jesus Christ.

Psalms 9:1

"I will praise thee, O Lord, with my whole heart; I will shew forth all thy marvelous works."

King David wrote the book of Psalms, and as the scripture shows us, had a lot to be thankful for. Despite his mistakes and there were some big ones, God still showed David His favor and considered him to be a man after his own heart. Sometimes it is hard to look at ourselves with our bad habits and messy lives, weaknesses and stumbling blocks, and find blessings. But a closer look will reveal we have been blessed immeasurably. Like David, when we realize how much the Lord has blessed us, we can't help but to love Him with our whole heart, the way He also loves us.

Proverbs 23:26

"My son, give me thine heart, and let thine eyes observe my ways."

This passage of scripture shows us God is looking for our heart. What is the heart if not the fountainhead of all human emotion? From the heart we feel both love and pain. God won't take our love against our will, rather He asks for it voluntarily. But, there is a test involved, and it comes with a choice on the part of the believer. Will we willingly submit to God, thereby giving Him our love and devotion, or will we flee from the union with our creator? To freely give our heart to God is to enjoin us to his will. In doing so, He will give us peace that surpasseth all understanding.

Matthew 5:16

"Let your light so shine before men, that they may see your good works, and glorify your Father which is in heaven."

In this scripture, the "light" is the indwelling of Jesus in our lives. It's that glorious light Jesus wants to be displayed for all to see. God wants our works to glorify Him and His kingdom. What we do in our daily lives reflects not just on us but back to God and the role He plays in our lives. Believers really are ambassadors for Jesus. We should remember the brief time a person may see us could influence not just the way they feel about us, but the way they feel about people of faith. It's easy to forget that. Knowing no, one is perfect and we all fail, we should strive to be diligent and to exemplify our hope and faith through our actions for the world around us to see.

Isaiah 6:8

"Also I heard the voice of the Lord, saying, whom shall I send, and who will go for us? Then said I, here am I; send me!"

Isaiah was given a task and not an easy one at that. He had to carry some bad news to the people of Israel, but he did it without question. How many of us stand up and volunteer when asked? What if it involves a difficult task like delivering bad news? God equipped Isaiah with strength and fortitude, and was with him every step of his journey. We should always remember we are never alone; God is always there with us no matter how difficult our tasks may be.

Acts 20:28

"Take heed therefore unto yourselves, and to all the flock, over the which the Holy Ghost hath made you overseers, to feed the church of God, which He hath purchased with his own blood."

The Apostle Paul is exhorting church leaders to be on their guard as there were uncertain times ahead. He tells them to not only watch after themselves but the local congregations of believers. Paul reminds the elders they are commissioned by the Holy Spirit to be leaders in their communities and to guide new followers of Jesus. When it comes to our own lives, we have responsibilities and are to watch how we act, what we think, and how we encourage others in faith. Each of us are charged never to forget we all have a part to play in God's church: a body of believers bought with His own precious blood.

Luke 9:23-24

"And He said to them all, if any man will come after me, let him deny himself, and take up his cross daily, and follow me. For whosoever will save his life shall lose it: but whosoever will lose his life for my sake, the same shall save it."

It's hard to deny ourselves. It's easy to follow our own ways. Jesus knows this. He knows us and our desire to follow our path more than his sometimes. To deny oneself requires great discipline and sacrifice. Learning to say "no" when we are used to telling ourselves "yes" is the trick. It won't happen overnight, but slowly learning to take ourselves out of the equation while letting God come into our lives more and more is the only way we will find ourselves on the same path as our savior.

Matthew 7:13-14

"Enter ye in at the strait gate: for wide is the gate, and broad is the way, that leadeth to destruction, and many there be which go in there at: because strait is the gate, and narrow is the way, which leadeth unto life, and few there be that find it."

This verse is often use to characterize the Christian life and the sometimes stoic adherence to God's word we must take in order to walk the narrow path. Most people including some who profess faith in Jesus will travel the path that leads to the wide gate. That's the easy path, one which leads to destruction and takes no effort to enter. However, it's that narrow gate we want to enter. Jesus knows this path is difficult which is why he describes it the way he does. We must always remember, our choices exercised through our free will, come with consequences which can affect our communion with our Lord.

Matthew 19:13-15

"Then were there brought unto Him little children, that He should put His hands on them, and pray: and the disciples rebuked them. But Jesus said, suffer little children, and forbid them not, to come unto me: for of such is the kingdom of heaven. And he laid His hands on them, and departed thence."

This passage paints an image of children: innocent, full of energy, boundless potential and with a full life ahead of them. There are parallels here between children and new believers. Both start out their lives (physical and then spiritual) uncorrupted by the world. But, as they age begin to pick up blemishes from the stain of sin in their lives. Regardless of how many blemishes they may have, when they turn to Jesus with a repentant heart, they are always welcomed them back. With outstretched arms, He renews them again and again, making them spotless through His grace poured out for all who would believe in Him.

James 1:19

"Blessed is the man that endureth temptation:
for when he is tried, he shall receive the crown of life, which the
Lord hath promised to them that love Him."

This passage of scripture emphasizes the importance of fortitude. The ability to stand strong in the face of uncertainty is a trait all Christians should strive to have.

The ability to overcome the barbs and snares of the devil, and to endure in our faith and belief in God despite those around us who may be pulling us down, is the test. The reward? A crown of life given to us by God because we both loved him and through his grace, overcame the evil one.

Micah 6:6-8

"Wherewith shall I come before the Lord, and bow myself before the high God? shall I come before Him with burnt offerings, with calves of a year old? Will the Lord be pleased with thousands of rams, or with ten thousands of rivers of oil? shall I give my firstborn for my transgression, the fruit of my body for the sin of my soul? He hath shewed thee, O man, what is good; and what doth the Lord require of thee, but to do justly, and to love mercy, and to walk humbly with thy God?"

Despite all the vain things we try to do to please God, all he wants for us is to love others and to be obedient to his holy word.

2 Corinthians 4:1

"Therefore seeing we have this ministry, as we have received mercy, we faint not;"

The Apostle Paul had a mission. That mission was to take the saving gospel of Jesus to the masses.

Paul was given this mission from God. Paul didn't feel worthy to carry the pure gospel message but knew it was God's will for him to do so. Through the many challenges, toils and snares he and others faced, he never lost heart.

We as believers all find a purpose through Jesus. We might not be preachers or teachers, but we have abilities and talents through which God's pure word can be distributed to others. Like Paul, we often feel inadequate to carry God's saving message. We wholly rely on God's strength and grace to see us through each day carrying His gospel in our hearts wherever we may go.

Psalms 118:6

"The Lord is on my side; I will not fear: what can man do unto me?"

King David, had many victories leading up to his writing this passage. He'd also faced many devastating challenges including the death of a child. While he had experienced many trials in his life, David still praised God and boldly proclaimed his faith regardless of what life brought him.

So many times, we face struggles and lack the confidence to tackle them head on. We can learn a lot from David and his reliance on God for his strength. We too can find assurance through our faith that God will see us through life's most difficult circumstances by placing our complete trust in Him.

Isaiah 40:28-31

"Hast thou not known? hast thou not heard, that the everlasting God, the Lord, the Creator of the ends of the earth, fainteth not, neither is weary? there is no searching of his understanding.

He giveth power to the faint; and to them that have no might He increaseth strength. Even the youths shall faint and be weary, and the young men shall utterly fall: But they that wait upon the Lord shall renew their strength; they shall mount up with wings as eagles; they shall run, and not be weary; and they shall walk, and not faint."

This scripture describes the relationship between a Christian and God through faith in Jesus and his sacrifice for their sins. It speaks of spiritual transformation. It forms the bridge connecting God's holy spirit with the believer who will serve as their spiritual guide throughout their lives. The bond of love between the creator and the created is also emphasized here: a bond offering the hope of eternal security and everlasting life for the believer faith and obedience to God's Holy Word.

1 John 4:15-16

"Whosoever shall confess that Jesus is the Son of God, God dwelleth in him, and he in God. And we have known and believed the love that God hath to us. God is love; and he that dwelleth in love dwelleth in God, and God in him."

This scripture describes the relationship between a Christian and God through faith in Jesus and His sacrifice for their sins. It speaks of spiritual transformation. It forms the bridge connecting God's holy spirit with the believer who will serve as their spiritual guide throughout their lives. The bond of love between the creator and the created is also emphasized here: a bond offering the hope of eternal security and everlasting life for the believer faith and obedience to God's Holy Word.

Galatians 5:13

"For, brethren, ye have been called unto liberty; only use not liberty for an occasion to the flesh, but by love serve one another."

This passage of scripture teaches us to appreciate the freedom God gives us through our faith in Jesus Christ and obedience to God's will for us; and to not take this freedom for granted. It's easy to become complacent with our freedom which can lead to carelessness in how we live our lives. The Apostle Paul is teaching his followers, and us, our freedom in Jesus is best used to honor Him with our lives and serve Him and others with humility and love.

1 Peter 5:7-9

"Casting all your care upon Him; for He careth for you.
Be sober, be vigilant; because your adversary the devil, as a roaring
lion, walketh about, seeking whom he may devour:
Whom resist stedfast in the faith, knowing that the same afflictions
are accomplished in your brethren that are in the world."

This scripture reminds us as believers to cast our anxieties on God. The Apostle Peter reminds his audience the devil takes delight in the suffering of Christians. Our anxieties and fears provide a path for the devil to enter in and tempt us, causing more doubt and fear. Relying on the strength of God's promises is the only way to live a life of peace.

2 Timothy 4:18

"And the Lord shall deliver me from every evil work, and will preserve me unto His heavenly kingdom: to whom be glory for ever and ever. Amen."

While in prison, the Apostle Paul faced persecution, rejection and loneliness. When he wrote this letter to Timothy, it was likely he was facing punishment, including death, for his preaching. Despite his bitter reality, Paul joyfully proclaimed his faith and trusted that God would see Him through it.

What is our response when we face great trials and tribulations? We as believers can have the same confidence Paul did as we lean in closer to God to see us through whatever difficulty we may face in this life.

Esther 4:14

"For if thou altogether holdest thy peace at this time, then shall there enlargement and deliverance arise to the Jews from another place; but thou and thy father 's house shall be destroyed: and who knoweth whether thou art come to the kingdom for such a time as this?

In this verse, Queen Esther was put in a position to try to influence the king to both spare her life and the lives of her people. She knew there was a possibility she could have died for her unsolicited petition in the king's court, but also knew if she didn't address the king, many could perish. Sometimes God puts us in places at times we don't understand, to do things we never thought we would, for the benefit of others and to bring glory to God's greater purpose in our lives.

Isaiah 43:2

"When thou passest through the waters, I will be with thee; and
through the rivers, they shall not overflow thee:
when thou walkest through the fire, thou shalt not be burned; neither
shall the flame kindle upon thee."

In this scripture, God reassured the Jewish people of His favor toward them. He was their confidence during trials and tribulations they faced each day. As He was to them, He is to us. Our heavenly father is the ever-present foundation providing confidence to believers that He will see them through life's challenges. This assurance is granted to all those who are members of God's family through faith in His son Jesus and His atoning sacrifice for our sins. It's that faith which anchors us in the enduring hope only God can give.

Psalms 55:2

"Cast thy burden upon the Lord, and He shall sustain thee: He shall never suffer the righteous to be moved."

Burdens, we all have them: health, finances, love...

Regardless of how they manifest in our lives, God tells us to let go of them and cast them at His feet. His sustaining power quenches our spiritual thirst when we are weak, and is what keeps us moving forward, one step at a time. God's promise He will not let the righteous be moved combines His ability to accept our burdens with His desire to sustain us, and keep us from ruin. It's the ultimate expression of God's love for His children, and the assurance we have that He will never let us slip from His hand if we place our complete trust in Him.

Ephesians 6:10

"Finally, my brethren, be strong in the Lord, and in the power of His might."

This passage teaches believers to always trust in God's strength and His ability to empower us to overcome difficulties we face in this life.

He, being the omnipotent creator of all things, knows where we succeed and where we struggle in our walk with Him. God and His union with each believer provide a constant source of strength for us, regardless of how weak we may feel. It's in our weakness that our love and need for God grows strongest. We need Him, and He reminds us He is always there to lift us up and see us through whatever twists and turns life may have in store.

Romans 8:26

"Likewise the Spirit also helpeth our infirmities: for we know not what we should pray for as we ought: but the Spirit itself maketh intercession for us with groanings which cannot be uttered."

Many times we struggle to find the words to say as we pray. Sometimes what we really need isn't exactly what we ask for. It's during those times the Holy Spirit intercedes on our behalf. Our reliance on God's spirit helps connect us to our father in Heaven in an intimate way: one of a child coming humbly to their father during their time of need.

Romans 12:4-5

"For as we have many members in one body, and all members have not the same office: So we, being many, are one body in Christ, and every one members one of another."

Here, Paul talks about the collective body of Christ and its many members. Membership in this universal church is based on one's faith and obedience to the gospel by obeying the will of God illustrated in His word. Each member has different talents and abilities, but collectively act on the will of God daily to bring honor and glory to His kingdom.

James 1:22

"But be ye doers of the word, and not hearers only, deceiving your own selves."

How often do we either see or hear instructions and fail to act? Probably more times that we would like to admit! James is instructing believers in a way to avoid ambivalence. He's telling his audience to take action with their faith and not just listen to the message. We should do the same in our lives by acting on what we read in scripture, applying it to our lives in order to live a life obedient to God.

Psalms 188:6

"The Lord is on my side; I will not fear: what can man do unto me?"

King David, had many victories leading up to his writing this passage. He'd also faced many devastating challenges including the death of a child. While he had experienced many trials in his life, David still praised God and boldly proclaimed his faith regardless of what life brought him. So many times, we face struggles and lack the confidence to tackle them head on. We can learn a lot from David and his reliance on God for his strength.

We too can find assurance through our faith that God will see us through life's most difficult circumstances by placing our complete trust in him.

Matthew 20:20-21

"And he saith unto them, whose is this imageand superscription? They say unto him, Caesar's. Then saith he unto them, Render therefore unto Caesar the things which are Caesar's;and unto God the things that are God's."

In this scripture, Jesus was answering a question with an obvious answer posed by the Pharisees who were trying to trap him. In his response, Jesus tells the gathered crowd to give what is owed to the government represented by Caesar because the coin bore his likeness.

There is another lesson. We should always be mindful of both God and government's role in our lives. Every day we should strive to live out our faith while at the same time, obeying laws intended to give society its order.

About The Author

Richard Tew is a journalist and author covering a wide range of topics from NASA to community news, to faith-based topics. He's regularly-published in The Post Newspaper in Galveston County, where he also produces faith-based media including podcasts and a daily radio segment "Our Daily Bread: A Daily Scripture and Reflection" heard on Patriot Talk 920 A.M. KYST in the Houston-Galveston region of Texas.

Richard enjoys interviewing faithful members of various Christian faith traditions from around the globe and has been enriched by visiting local churches in traditions not his own in order to learn how others celebrate and commemorate their relationship to their savior.

A life-long member of Watters Road Church of Christ, Richard along with his family have attended Watters for 43 years.

When he is not working on his next media project, Richard teaches Irish dance to students of all ages in the Clear Lake, TX area.